JOKES TO
TELL THE
QUEEN

Really quite amusing!

Dedicated with great affection to
Her Majesty the Queen.
We hope we make you smile.

Bloomsbury Publishing, London, Berlin, New York and Sydney

First published in Great Britain in 1996 by Bloomsbury Publishing Plc
50 Bedford Square, London, WC1B 3DP

This revised edition first published in June 2012

The 1996 edition was edited by Caroline Plaisted

A CIP catalogue record for this book is available from the British Library

ISBN 978 1 4088 3246 2

1 3 5 7 9 10 8 6 4 2

Typeset by Hewer Text UK Ltd
Printed in Great Britain by Clays Ltd, St Ives plc, Bungay, Suffolk

www.bloomsbury.com

JOKES TO TELL THE QUEEN

BLOOMSBURY

LONDON BERLIN NEW YORK SYDNEY

CONTENTS

INTRODUCTION

Can you imagine what it must be like to be the Queen? She has lots more pocket money than you'll ever have, uses special aircraft and trains, and owns many massive houses. Unlike you, she's got servants who make breakfast for her and clean out her bedroom. If she wants to go somewhere, she has a chauffeur to drive her car – and who will wash it afterwards if it gets muddy.

On the other hand, not only does the Queen have to rule the United Kingdom but she is also Head of the Commonwealth. So, wherever she goes, the Queen has to speak to people, be nice to them, shake their hands and smile all the time – even if she's got toothache or a bunged-up nose!

Her Royal Highness the Princess Elizabeth was born on 21st April 1926 and she was crowned Queen Elizabeth II on 2nd June 1953. After thinking about all the hard work the Queen has to do, and to celebrate her Diamond Jubilee (marking 60 years of the Queen's reign), we thought we'd put together all of your favourite jokes which you told us that you'd like to tell the Queen if you got to meet her. After all, everyone needs a laugh to make them happy. So why not turn the page and celebrate with the Queen and with a chuckle?

CORGI CHUCKLES
AND OTHER
ANIMAL JOKES

Everyone knows that the Queen loves animals — she keeps corgis and Labradors and has lots of horses, some of which are race horses. These jokes are guaranteed to have the Queen and her corgis chuckling.

Why do French people eat snails?
Because they don't like fast food.

Why couldn't Batman go fishing?
Because Robin had eaten all the worms.

What's round and furry and smells of mint?
A polo bear.

What's round, made of chocolate and sits on the seabed?
An oyster egg.

The Queen once had a parrot and if she pulled his right leg he said prayers. If she pulled his left leg he said grace. One day, a priest came along and said, 'I wonder what would happen if I pulled both legs?'
The parrot replied, 'I'd fall off my perch, idiot!'

Why do goats wear bells?
Because their horns don't work.

What do you call a deer with no eyes?
No eye deer . . .

What does a cat say if you stand on its tail?
Mee-ouch!

What's black and white and red all over?
A sunburned penguin.

When do elephants paint their toenails red?
When they want to hide in the cherry tree.

What's the difference between a piano and a fish?
You can't tune a fish!

What do you call married horses?
A bridle and groom.

How many Fs are in this: a farmer found a fox in a field?
None — there are no Fs in 'this'.

What do you call a sheep with no legs?
A cloud.

Where do you go if you need a pat
on the head?
Under a cow.

How do you stop the corgi from barking in the back garden?
Put him in the front garden.

What goes *oom oom*?
A cow walking backwards.

How do you know if an elephant has been in the fridge?
By the footprints in the butter.

Why did the one-eyed bird cross the road?
To get to the bird's eye shop.

What pet does the Queen keep in her loo?
The privy seal.

What's the best thing to do if your corgi
swallows a dictionary?
Take the words right out of his mouth.

A horse walks into a shop and the shopkeeper says,
'What's with the long face?'

What do you get if you cross a cow with a camel?
A lumpy milkshake.

What do corgis do in cold weather?
Sit around the fire.

What do corgis do in very cold weather?
Light the fire.

What would happen if the Queen had a cow, a duck and
a goat?
*She'd have cream quackers and cheese for breakfast
every day.*

What do you get if you pour hot water down a rabbit
hole?
Hot cross bunnies.

How do you hire a horse?
Put it on four bricks.

What does a man do standing up, a woman sitting down and a corgi on three legs?
Shake hands.

What do you get if you cross a sheep with a kangaroo?
A woolly jumper.

What do Henry the Eighth and Kermit the Frog have in common?
The.

What goes *99-bonk?*
A centipede with a wooden leg.

Why couldn't the two elephants go swimming?
Because they only had one pair of trunks.

What bull sleeps?
A bulldozer.

What's the difference between a dog and a flea?
A dog can have fleas but a flea can't have dogs.

What do birds eat for breakfast?
Tweetabix.

What did the dog say when it sat on sandpaper?
Ruff, ruff!

What is black and white and noisy?
A penguin playing the drums.

What do you call a dog on a warm day?
A hot dog.

What's a crocodile's favourite game?
Snap.

What do you call a short-sighted dinosaur?
I don't think he saw us. (Say it fast.)

Why aren't there any pills in the jungle?
Because the parrots-eat-'em-all.

What computer game do animals play in the jungle?
Mortal Wombat.

Which American city has lots of cows?
Moo York.

Why did the hedgehog say 'ouch'?
Because his prickles were inside out.

What is a cow's favourite game?
Moosical chairs.

What do you call a fish with a fishing rod?
A fishing fish.

How do pigs dress?
In mud.

What do you call a cat sitting on a log?
A catalogue!

Why did the dinosaur have spots?
Because it had chicken pox.

What goes up slowly and comes down fast?
An elephant in a lift.

What do you call an elephant that can't do sums?
Dumbo.

What animals in Noah's Ark didn't come in pairs?
Worms – they came in apples.

Why do bees fly with their legs crossed?
Because they are looking for the BP station.

Why is a turkey like a cushion?
Because it is full of stuffing.

What do you get if you cross a snowman with a man-eating shark?
Frostbite.

What do you call a stag with no eyes?
Still no idea!

What happened when the pig took up flying lessons?
The price of bacon went up.

What goes to bed with its shoes on?
A horse.

Why did one snake ask the other snake if it
was poisonous?
Because it bit him!

Why did the hedgehog cross the road?
To see his flat mate.

Which fly makes films?
Steven Spielbug.

What did Pink Panther say when he stood on an ant?
*'Dead ant, dead ant, dead ant, dead ant, dead ant, dead
ant, dead ant, dead ant, dead ant ...' (Sing it to the theme
tune!)*

Ten cats were on a boat and one cat jumped off. How
many cats were left?
None – the others were copycats.

Why did the pop star cross the road?
Because he was stapled to the chicken.

Why do bees hum?
Because they don't know the words.

What do cows drink?
Mooshakes.

What do you get if you cross a tiger and a sheep?
A stripy woolly.

Why did the tortoise cross the road?
Because he wanted to get to the Shell station.

What do you get if you cross a hare and a cow?
A hairy cow.

What did the dinosaur say to the elephant?
Nothing – they can't talk.

What did the grape do when the elephant sat on it?
Gave a little whine.

Why did the lobster blush?
Because the seaweed.

How do you keep flies out of the kitchen?
Put all the rubbish in the living room.

What's the best way to stop fish smelling?
Cut off their noses.

What's the difference between Indian and African elephants?
About 3,000 miles.

How do you weigh a whale?
At a whale weigh station.

Why did the cow laugh when he slipped on the ice?
Because it's no use crying over spilt milk.

What's a slug?
A snail with a housing problem.

What do you give a sick pig?
Oinkment.

Where do you send a sick wasp?
Waspital.

Why did the cow cross the road?
Because it was the chicken's day off.

Why did the dinosaur cross the forest?
Because roads hadn't been invented then!

How does an octopus go into battle?
Well armed.

What is a sheep's favourite doll?
Barrrrbie.

Why did the chewing gum cross the road?
Because it got stuck to the chicken's foot.

What animals need oiling?
Mice – because they squeak.

Why do tigers eat raw meat?
Because they don't know how to cook.

Why do birds fly south in winter?
Because it's too far to walk.

Why does a lion wear a furry coat?
Because he'd look stupid in a raincoat.

What's worse than a giraffe with a sore throat?
A centipede with blisters.

How do you know if carrots are good for your eyesight?
Have you ever seen a rabbit wearing glasses?

What do you do if there is a gorilla in your bed?
Sleep somewhere else!

Why did the piggy cross the road?
To get to the piggy bank.

Who is the Queen of hares and rabbits?
Hare Majesty.

What goes *tick, tock, woof, woof*?
A watchdog.

How do you communicate with a fish?
Drop it a line.

Where does a horse go when it's ill?
Horsepital.

What's the fastest fish in the world?
A motor pike.

What's black and white and runs on
sixteen wheels?
A zebra on roller skates.

TEA TRIP

If you invited the Queen to tea and she wrote back saying she was coming, have you any idea what you'd give her to eat? Would it be Coronation Chicken washed down with Queen Anne tea? Or Palatial Plaice followed by Royal Trifle or Queen of Puddings?

My Royal Tea Menu would be:

This is what I would talk to the Queen about:

The other guests at tea would be:

ROYAL TEA ETIQUETTE

1 You should send your invitation to: *The Private Secretary to Her Majesty the Queen, Buckingham Palace, London.*

2 When the Queen arrives at your house, wait until she offers you her hand before you shake it.

3 Bow or curtsy when you say 'Good afternoon, Your Majesty'.

4 When the Queen speaks to you for the first time, reply and call her 'Your Majesty'. After that, you can call her 'Ma'am' (say it like 'Marm').

5 You'll need to lay a place at the table for either the Queen's Lady-in-Waiting or her Private Secretary and also the police officer who accompanies the Queen to protect her.

6 The Queen is the guest of honour so make sure she has the best seat.

7 None of your guests should leave until the Queen has gone home.

PRACTICAL TIP NUMBER 1

How to Hold a Handbag

1 Never use a bag with a shoulder strap – with all that hand-shaking and waving it will keep sliding down your arm. Instead you need a large bag with small handles.

2 Holding it is easy – just hook the handles over your wrist and then draw your elbow into your wrist like in this picture.

3 Do your best to hold the bag like this all day. (The Queen has to, so why shouldn't you!)

PALATIAL PROFESSORS
AND OTHER SCHOOL SQUEALERS

Even though the Queen wasn't sent to school, she had to work hard with her private tutor at home. She probably worked harder than the biggest swot in your school because the teacher was never distracted by anyone else.

We reckon that the Queen deserves a good laugh!

TEACHER: What nuts can you hang pictures on?
PUPIL: Walnuts.

TEACHER: What has a head and a tail but no body?
PUPIL: A penny, miss.

TEACHER: If I laid two eggs on one side of the table and two on the other, how many would I have?
PUPIL: I don't know, sir, but I'd like to see you try it.

TEACHER: If I had four apples in one hand and five oranges in the other, what would I have?
PUPIL: Big hands, miss!

TEACHER: Where does the Queen keep her armies?
PUPIL: Up her sleevies, sir.

TEACHER: What do Italians play at parties?
PUPIL: Pasta parcel.

TEACHER: What do you call a woman covered in yellow grease?
PUPIL: Marge!

TEACHER: What do you call a man with a spade on his head?
PUPIL: Doug.

TEACHER: Where is Hadrian's Wall?
PUPIL: Around Hadrian's house, miss.

TEACHER: Why does the word 'lady' need a 'y'?
PUPIL: Because if it didn't have one it would be a lad!

TEACHER: Why does the Queen
employ beefeaters?
PUPIL: Because she likes their
burgers.

TEACHER: What do you call a
man with a plank on his head?
PUPIL: Edwood.

TEACHER: Why did the clown wear a red nose?
PUPIL: To make him look funny, miss.

TEACHER: Where does the Queen keep her loose change?
PUPIL: In the Bank of England.

TEACHER: What's the difference
between a ball and a prince?
PUPIL: One is thrown in the air and
the other is heir to the throne.

TEACHER: What can be found all over
the house?
PUPIL: A roof, sir.

TEACHER: What does the Queen use when she gets a
puncture?
PUPIL: A Union Jack!

TEACHER: Where does the Queen come from?
PUPIL: Alaska.
TEACHER: No, don't bother. I'll ask her myself.

TEACHER: What's the worst thing to find in a second-hand shop?
PUPIL: A toilet roll.

TEACHER: What runs around Buckingham Palace but can't move?
PUPIL: The perimeter wall.

TEACHER: How do you make a band stand?
PUPIL: Take away their chairs, sir.

TEACHER: Why did the bald man go for a walk?
PUPIL: To get some fresh hair.

TEACHER: Where does the Queen play tennis?
PUPIL: On the Crown Court.

TEACHER: Which are the poshest ski resorts?
PUPIL: The ones covered in royal icing.

TEACHER: What does the Queen drink?
PUPIL: Royal tea.

TEACHER: What was the first thing Queen Elizabeth did when she came to the throne?
PUPIL: Sit on it.

TEACHER: Which hand does the Queen use to stir her tea?
PUPIL: She doesn't – she uses her spoon like everyone else!

TEACHER: What's the difference between the Queen and a storm?
PUPIL: The Queen reigns longer.

PUPIL: Do you notice any change in me?
TEACHER: Why?
PUPIL: I've just swallowed my bus fare.

TEACHER: What do you get if you drop butter on the floor?
PUPIL: Flora, miss.

TEACHER: What kind of cheese is made backwards?
PUPIL: Edam.

TEACHER: Which English king invented the fireplace?
PUPIL: Alfred the Great!

TEACHER: What's the sport of Queens?
PUPIL: Windsor-fing.

TEACHER: How many letters are there in the alphabet?
PUPIL: 24, sir.
TEACHER: Why?
PUPIL: Because I have a letter saying I have to miss PE.

TEACHER: Why wouldn't the Queen make a good teacher?
PUPIL: Because she doesn't know all her subjects.

TEACHER: How do you make a sausage roll?
PUPIL: Push it down the hill.

TEACHER: Who invented fire?
PUPIL: Oh, some bright spark.

TEACHER: Why did the Queen throw the clock out of the window?
PUPIL: To see time fly.

TEACHER: What does the Queen keep bottles closed with?
PUPIL: Corkies.

TEACHER: Why did the Queen say 'ouch' when she walked into the bar?
PUPIL: Because it was a metal bar!

TEACHER: Why does the Queen wave her right hand?
PUPIL: Because the left one's mine!

TEACHER: Why did the Queen bring a hammer to school?
PUPIL: Because they were breaking up.

TEACHER: You missed school yesterday, didn't you?
PUPIL: No, I didn't miss it one bit!

TEACHER: Why did the robber have a bath?
PUPIL: Because he wanted to make a clean getaway.

TEACHER: What's frozen water?
PUPIL: Ice.
TEACHER: What's frozen tea?
PUPIL: Iced tea.
TEACHER: What's frozen cream?
PUPIL: Ice cream.
TEACHER: What's frozen ink?
PUPIL: Iced ink.
TEACHER: Well, have a bath then!

TEACHER: How do you start a teddy-bear race?
PUPIL: Ready, teddy, go!

TEACHER: What's 300 metres high and wobbles?
PUPIL: The Trifle Tower.

TEACHER: What do you call a woman with two lavatories?
PUPIL: Lulu.

TEACHER: What says 'Now you see me, now you don't, now you see me, now you don't'?
PUPIL: A snowman on a zebra crossing!

TEACHER: What goes up but never comes down?
PUPIL: Your age.

TEACHER: How can you cut the sea?
PUPIL: With a sea-saw.

TEACHER: What month has 28 days?
PUPIL: All of them!

PUPIL: Should you write with your left hand or your right hand?
TEACHER: Neither – you should write with a pen.

TEACHER: What's the difference between a fireman and a soldier?
PUPIL: Well, you can't dip a fireman in your egg.

TEACHER: Why are goldfish orange?
PUPIL: Because the water makes them rusty.

TEACHER: What flies and wobbles?
PUPIL: A jellycopter.

TEACHER: How do you stay cool at a football match?
PUPIL: Stand next to a fan.

TEACHER: What do you call a man with eight bala-
clavas on his head?
PUPIL: Anything you like – he won't hear you!

TEACHER: What happened to the plant in the maths
lesson?
PUPIL: It grew square roots.

TEACHER: In which battle did Nelson die?
PUPIL: His last one.

What did the cross-eyed teacher say?
'I can't control my pupils.'

PRACTICAL TIP NUMBER 2

What to Keep in Your Handbag

Exactly what the Queen keeps in her handbag is a secret, but the following items would probably come in useful in your own handbag:

- A handkerchief (for blowing your royal nose)

- A lipstick in Balmoral Red (because your lipstick will quickly wear away with all the talking you need to do!)

- A list of things to do (so that you don't forget who you're meant to visit next)

- An iPod (so you won't get bored on the journey home)

- A torch (in case the lights go out)

- A packet of sweeties (in case you get hungry)

- A plastic bag (to put your leftover food in so that you can take it home to the corgis)

 A pair of gloves (in case you have to shake hands with someone who has sticky hands)

 A notebook (so that you can write down what you're going to get everyone for Christmas)

 A pencil or pen (to do all your writing with)

Can you think of anything else which you would find useful?

FANTASY ROYAL FAMILY

Everyone, at some stage, has tried to imagine what it must be like to be the Queen. But can you imagine what it would be like if your family actually were the Royal Family? Do you think they'd be any good at it? Do you think your dad would make a better Prince of Wales or a Duke of Edinburgh? Would your auntie be better than your granny as the Duchess of Cornwall or Princess Anne?

Why not have some fun matching your family to the royal one to create your very own Fantasy Royal Family!

REAL ROYAL FAMILY   FANTASY ROYAL FAMILY

THE QUEEN. . . . .

THE DUKE OF EDINBURGH . . . .

THE PRINCE OF WALES . . . .

THE DUCHESS OF CORNWALL. . . . .

THE PRINCESS ROYAL. . . . .

THE DUKE OF YORK. . . . .

THE EARL OF WESSEX. . . . .

THE DUKE OF CAMBRIDGE . . . .

THE DUCHESS OF CAMBRIDGE. . . . .

PRINCE HARRY. . . . .

THE CORGIS . . . .

ROYAL RIB-TICKLERS
AND OTHER FAMILY HOWLERS

The Queen has a very large family and invites them to stay with her as often as possible. Don't you think she deserves to get her own back on them by telling some of these jokes?

Why did the hand cross the road?
To get to the second-hand shop.

What do sea monsters like to eat?
Fish and ships.

What is red and stupid?
A blood clot.

What happened to the man who always wore sunglasses?
He took a very dim view of things.

What's the last thing you take off before going to bed?
Your feet – off the floor.

Why do Eskimos eat candles?
For light refreshment.

When does a bed change size?
At night – when two feet are added.

What's the fastest cake in the world?
Scone!

What did the traffic lights say to the sports car?
Don't look now – I'm changing.

Why didn't the skeleton go to the party?
Because it had no body to go with.

Why didn't the milkman get an OBE?
Because he had lost his bottle.

QUEEN: Arise, Sir Gavin, you are now a knight.
SIR GAVIN: Can I have a moon to go with the night? I'm afraid of the dark.

What did the referee say to the pushy snooker player?
'Go to the back of the cue!'

PATIENT: Doctor, Doctor – I think I'm a goat!
DOCTOR: How long has this been going on?
PATIENT: Since I was a kid.

Did you hear about the tap dancer?
She broke her leg when she fell in the sink.

Why did the orange cross the road?
Because he wanted to be orange squash.

What's yellow and goes up and down?
A banana in a lift.

What did the big chimney say to the little chimney?
You're too young to smoke.

What do you say if a biscuit gets run over?
Crumbs!

MAN: Please can I have some helicopter crisps?
SHOPKEEPER: Sorry, we've only got plane.

What's green and hairy and goes up and down?
A gooseberry in a lift.

What happens if the Queen burps at her birthday party?
She issues a royal pardon.

DOCTOR: Did you drink a glass of orange juice after your bath?
PATIENT: No – after drinking the bath I didn't fancy the orange juice.

What did the big candle say to the little candle?
I'm going out tonight.

What did the Queen say on the 1st January?
Happy New Year!

What's the Queen's favourite game?
A game of chess – because she knows all the moves.

What do skeletons eat off?
Bone china plates.

What did the Queen's astronauts see in their kitchen?
Unidentified Frying Objects.

Why does the Queen wave her hand?
Because if she nodded her head her crown would fall off.

What would you do if you met a cannibal?
Give him a hand.

BOY: Can you pull a rabbit out of your hat?
MAGICIAN: No – I washed my hare last night and I can't do a thing with it.

MAN IN BUS QUEUE: How long will the next bus be?
ANOTHER MAN: About 11 metres, the same as the rest.

Why did the skeleton cross the road?
To get to the Body Shop.

What is big and ugly and covered with spots?
A monster with chicken pox.

'Polly, put the kettle on!'
'No – I don't think it would suit me.'

What did the King say to the hangman?
No noose is good noose.

What did the salad say to the fridge?
Close that door – I'm dressing.

What does a policeman have for dinner?
Truncheon meat.

What's green and goes camping?
A boy sprout.

Why didn't the Queen cross the potato patch?
Because she was afraid the eyes would look up her skirt.

What does the Queen do in her boat?
She waves.

PATIENT: Doctor, Doctor – I feel like a pair of curtains!
DOCTOR: Oh, shut up and pull yourself together!

Why was the pharaoh confused?
Because his daddy was a mummy.

What did the Queen's policeman say to his tummy?
You're under a vest.

Why did the Queen sit on the clock?
Because she wanted to be on time for her party.

Why is the sea always restless?
Because it's got so many rocks in its bed.

What did one eye say to the other eye?
Something between us smells.

Why did the weeping willow weep?
Because it saw the pine tree pine.

Why do you need an umbrella when you see the Queen?
Because wherever she goes she's always reigning.

What can the Queen say without saying anything?
Anything but ANYTHING.

Where does the Queen have her parties?
In the Houses of Partyment.

Why did the golfer have four shoes?
In case there was a hole in one.

Why does the Queen never race?
Because she is Queen Elizabeth the Second.

What does the Queen eat at birthday parties?
Royal jelly.

Why did the skeleton burp?
Because he didn't have the guts to fart.

What do two oceans say when they meet?
Nothing — they just wave.

CUSTOMER: Waiter, Waiter – this soup tastes funny.
WAITER: Why aren't you laughing then?

What is a net?
Holes tied together with string.

What do you call a girl with a frog on her head?
Lily.

How do you flatten a ghost?
With a spirit level.

What does the robot's tombstone say?
Rust in peace.

PATIENT: Doctor, Doctor – I feel like a cricket ball!
DOCTOR: Howzat?
PATIENT: Don't you start!

What do you call Postman Pat when he's sacked?
Pat.

What did the biscuits say to the almonds?
You're nuts and we're crackers.

Where does the Queen keep her knights' armour?
On her knights!

Why did the tomato blush?
Because it saw the salad dressing.

Where does the vampire keep his money?
At the blood bank.

What do you get if you cross a skunk with a boomerang?
A smell that's hard to get rid of.

What do you call two robbers?
A pair of knickers.

If an Earl is made an OBE, does he become an Earlobe?

Why did the skeleton run up the tree?
Because the dog was after his bones.

PRACTICAL TIP NUMBER 3

How to Wave

This is easy – but only if you have to do it for a short while.

Bend your elbow and raise your hand up towards your face. Now, keeping your elbow in at your waist, waggle your hand from side to side. Don't forget to keep smiling at the same time!

This waving is most often done while sitting in the back of a car and looking out of a window.

PRACTICAL TIP
NUMBER 4

How to Take a Corgi for a Walk

1 Find a corgi.

2 Attach a lead to the corgi's collar.

3 Put on a headscarf, an anorak and green wellies (see Practical Tip Number 6 for help with this).

4 Walk around your garden with the corgi.

5 Return to the house and give the corgi some food.

6 Remove your headscarf, anorak and wellies.

7 Sit down to watch *Coronation Street*.

POSH PALACES

Buckingham Palace has been standing for over 300 years and has many draughty rooms (775 of them!) and corridors. If you were the Queen or King you might find that you'd want to carry out a number of home improvements to make everything cosier.

Imagine if you had the chance to design a royal palace from scratch. What special features would you put in? How many bedrooms would you want? Would you want your own private cinema? Or perhaps you'd have a heated indoor swimming pool? Would you fit escalators so you don't have to climb the stairs? Or solar panels to save on the earth's resources?

There's lots of space at the end of the book to design your very own palace. Remember that you'll need to do a floor plan for each of the floors in your palace and it would be best if you name each of the rooms as you go.

NOBLE BUT NO BELL?
AND OTHER JOKES FOR SOMEONE WHO LIVES IN A HOUSE WITHOUT A DOORBELL

Because the Queen always arrives home in a chauffeur-driven car or a coach, she doesn't carry a house key. And no one knocks on her front door – everyone uses the side entrances. But the Queen is bound to appreciate a good knock, knock joke!

Knock, knock!
Who's there?
Isabel.
Isabel who?
Isabel necessary on a bike?

Knock, knock!
Who's there?
Doctor.
Doctor who?
Ah, so you did recognise me then.

Knock, knock!
Who's there?
Spell.
Spell who?
Oh, all right then. W-H-O.

Knock, knock!
Who's there?
Hawaii.
Hawaii who?
I'm fine. Hawaii you?

Knock, knock!
Who's there?
Heave.
Heave who?
Heave who, my hearties.

Knock, knock!
Who's there?
Lettuce.
Lettuce who?
Lettuce in and you'll find out.

Knock, knock!
Who's there?
Pencil.
Pencil who?
Pencil Sharpener.

Knock, knock!
Who's there?
Nana.
Nana who?
Nana your business!

Knock, knock!
Who's there?
Handsome.
Handsome who?
Handsome keys through the letter box or let me in!

Knock, knock!
Who's there?
Cows go.
Cows go who?
No – cows go moo!

Knock, knock!
Who's there?
Lettuce.
Lettuce who?
Lettuce in – I'm hungry!

Knock, knock!
Who's there?
Spook.
Spook who?
Spooketti Bolognese.

Knock, knock!
Who's there?
Police.
Police who?
I'm just a policeman. Now open the door or I'll have to knock it down.

Knock, knock!
Who's there?
Purr.
Purr who?
Purrhaps I could come into your party?

Knock, knock!
Who's there?
Boo.
Boo who?
There's no need to cry.

Knock, knock!
Who's there?
David.
David who?
David the doorbell so I had to knock.

Knock, knock!
Who's there?
Night.
Night who?
Goodnight to you too!

Knock, knock!
Who's there?
Granny.
Granny who?
Knock, knock!
Who's there?
Granny.
Granny who?
Knock, knock!
Who's there?
Granny.
Granny WHO?
Knock, knock!
Who's there?
Auntie.
Auntie who?
Auntie glad Granny's gone now?

Knock, knock!
Who's there?
You.
You who?
Yes — what do you want?

Knock, knock!
Who's there?
Hatch.
Hatch who?
Bless you!

Knock, knock!
Who's there?
Irish Stew.
Irish Stew who?
Irish Stew in the name of the law!

Knock, knock!
Who's there?
Ablieve.
Ablieve who?
Ablieve in Father Christmas.

Knock, knock!
Who's there?
Pudding.
Pudding who?
Pudding on your hat when it's raining is a good idea.

Knock, knock!
Who's there?
Banana.
Banana who?
Banana stew!

Knock, knock!
Who's there?
Will you remember me tomorrow?
Yes!
Knock, knock!
Who's there?
Will you remember me next week?
Yes!
Knock, knock!
Who's there?
You said you'd remember me!

Knock, knock!
Who's there?
Apple.
Apple who?
Apple stew!

Knock, knock!
Who's there?
Kanga.
Kanga who?
No – kangaroo!

Knock, knock!
Who's there?
Orange.
Orange who?
Orange you glad I didn't ring the bell?

Knock, knock!
Who's there?
Banana.
Banana who?
Knock, knock!
Who's there?
Banana.
Banana who?
Knock, knock!
Who's there?
Orange.
Orange who?
Orange you glad I didn't say banana?

Knock, knock!
Who's there?
Scott.
Scott who?
Scott nothing to do with you.

PRACTICAL TIP NUMBER 5

How to Wear a Crown without it Falling off

This requires lots of practice! It's worth watching any films or TV programmes which show the Queen at the State Opening of Parliament to pick up some tips.

If you can't borrow a crown from someone, you could try making one out of cardboard or you could see if anyone has a crown left over from their Christmas cracker. Alternatively, place a large hardback book on your head – after all, the real crown is very heavy! You'll need to stand in front of a mirror and then carefully balance your crown on top of your head.

Now walk slowly and regally around the room, remembering to look up at all times so that your crown doesn't slip. Once you can do this, try waving and shaking someone's hand while you're wearing your crown (see Practical Tip Number 3 for help with this).

QUEENLY QUIZ
(OR KINGLY KLUES)

How do you think you'd perform as the monarch? Answer this quiz to test your regal resources! Keep a note of your score so that you can see how you did at the end.

1 YOU'RE DUE TO CARRY OUT A VISIT IN AN OPEN-TOPPED HORSE-DRAWN CARRIAGE. THE PROBLEM IS THAT IT'S RAINING.

Do you:
A Cancel the trip and stay at home to watch a DVD.
B Put on a hat and raincoat and go anyway.
C Attend the event in a car instead.

2 IT'S TIME TO REVIEW THE ROYAL FINANCES.

Do you:
A Ask Parliament to give you a pay rise but no one else, and get the palace redecorated.
B Ask for more money for all your staff.
C Say that times are hard and that everyone, including you, can cope without any extra cash this year.

3 YOU'RE PLANNING YOUR DIARY AND REALISE YOU'VE BEEN INVITED TO AN OLD PEOPLE'S HOME, A FILM PREMIERE AND THE OPENING OF A NEW SCHOOL ALL ON THE SAME DAY.

Do you:
A Decide to go to the film premiere and say that you'll try to fit the rest in some other time.
B Arrange to visit the school in the morning, the old people's home in the afternoon and the film premiere in the evening.

C Say you'll go to the school and the old people's home but ask for a DVD of the film to watch at home.

4 YOU NEED TO ORDER A NEW SET OF FORMAL ROBES.

Do you:
A Pop out to the local department store and buy something off the peg.
B Arrange for a national competition to design and make the robes, giving student designers a chance to make their name.
C Go to your usual dress designer for their expert advice.

5 IT'S TIME TO RECORD YOUR TRADITIONAL CHRISTMAS BROADCAST.

Do you:
A Invite the recording crew to have tea in the staff cafeteria.
B Stay after the recording to have tea and mince pies with the crew.
C Offer them a special tea but have your own tea in your private rooms.

SEE NEXT PAGE FOR THE ANSWERS . . .

QUIZ ANSWERS

IF YOU ANSWERED MOSTLY As:

We don't think you'd last very long in charge — you're too selfish! In fact, monarchs like you ended up in the Tower of London not so long ago. We suggest that you abdicate.

IF YOU ANSWERED MOSTLY Bs:

It sounds like you're made of the right stuff to survive as ruler because you make everyone feel equally important and are prepared to put in a hard day's work. Your crown certainly won't slip.

IF YOU ANSWERED MOSTLY Cs:

You're usually on the right track but occasionally you're tempted to think about your own comfort first. Several years' more experience will teach you all you need to know.

PRACTICAL TIP NUMBER 6

How to Wear the Queen's Country Outfit

This outfit is essential for royal outings to the country and for corgi walking (see Practical Tip Number 4 for help with this).

👑 The Headscarf

1 Fold a square headscarf in half diagonally.
2 Put it over your head as shown.
3 Then tie a knot in the scarf under your chin. (This is known as a Knightsbridge Knot.)

👑 The Anorak

Ideally the anorak should be navy blue or dark green although an old skiing jacket would also do. Make sure the poppers are done up at all times. It's best worn with your hands in your pockets.

👑 The Wellies

These must be green – but not bright green. You might just get away with black ones.

PRACTICAL TIP NUMBER 7

How to Talk to Strangers during a Royal Visit

The ability to do this really successfully can only be acquired with years of practice – after all, the Queen's been doing it for 60 years! But here are some handy phrases which might help you get by:

👑 'Hello!'

👑 'Have you travelled far?'

👑 'Oh, really?'

👑 'How very interesting!'

👑 'Gosh – did you make it yourself?'

👑 'It was so nice to meet you.'

👑 'Thank you for coming.'

👑 'Goodbye!'

PRACTICAL TIP NUMBER 8

How to Prevent Your Feet from Aching on Walkabouts

1 Never wear high heels.

2 Make sure that your shoes fit properly.

3 Wear socks, not bare feet, inside your shoes on hot days.

4 Avoid getting chilblains by keeping warm!

5 Always have clean and sweet-smelling feet!

6 Sit down every now and then.

WHAT RULES WOULD YOU MAKE IF YOU WERE THE QUEEN (OR KING)?

If it was up to you, what special law would you pass for children? Would you declare that everyone should be given a free bag of sweets on the days that have the letter D in them? Or would you say that no one has to go to school on the days they have maths? Now you have the chance to write down your own List of Rules for Your Kingdom!

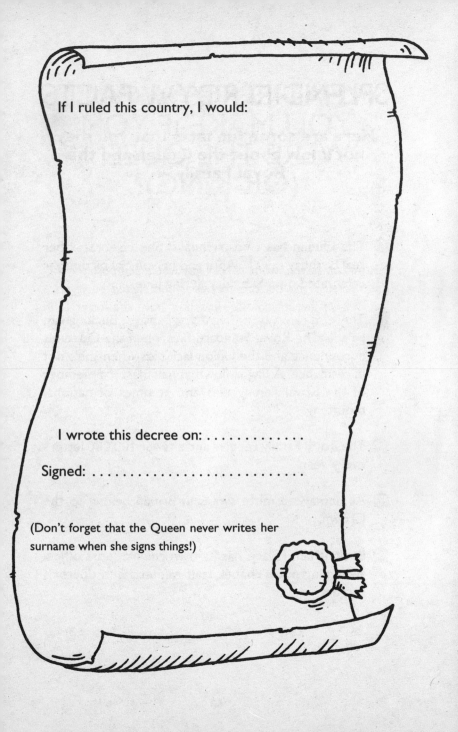

If I ruled this country, I would:

I wrote this decree on: . . . .

Signed: . . . .

(Don't forget that the Queen never writes her surname when she signs things!)

SPLENDID ROYAL FACTS

Here are some fun facts that you may not know about the Queen and the Royal Family . . .

👑 The Queen has two birthdays! She celebrates her real birthday on 21st April and her official birthday is celebrated on a Saturday during June.

👑 There is always a flag flying above Buckingham Palace. The Royal Standard flies when the Queen is in residence and the Union Jack flies when she's not in residence. A flag is flown at half mast if a member of the Royal Family dies and at times of national mourning.

👑 The Royal Family receive and answer 100,000 letters every year!

👑 All unmarked mute swans in Britain belong to the Crown.

👑 Buckingham Palace has its own cinema, post office, swimming pool, chapel, staff cafeteria and doctor's surgery.

The Queen doesn't need a British passport when she travels abroad! This is because British passports are issued in the name of Her Majesty. The rest of the Royal Family do have passports.

There are 775 rooms, 1,514 doors and 760 windows in Buckingham Palace. The windows are cleaned every six weeks!

The Queen rides a horse nearly every day when she stays at her country residences – even when it's raining.

The Royal Family has so much gold, silver and crockery that it employs the Yeoman of the Gold and Silver Pantry and the Yeoman of the Glass and China to look after it.

The Queen never went to school! Instead she had lessons at home with her sister, Princess Margaret.

The Royal Family carry out 2,000 official engagements every year, at home and overseas!

In the days when lions and leopards were kept at the Tower of London, there used to be a Keeper of the Lions.

The Queen keeps racing pigeons on her Sandringham Estate in Norfolk.

👑 Buckingham Palace wasn't used as a royal palace until 1837.

👑 An armed policeman stands guard outside the Queen's bedroom throughout the night.

👑 The Keeper of the Privy Purse is the man in charge of the royal housekeeping money.

👑 The Queen wears the Imperial State Crown at the State Opening of Parliament.

👑 You can't sue the Queen or take her to court – because the court belongs to the Queen!

👑 The Imperial State Crown is studded with 2,868 diamonds, 273 pearls, 17 sapphires, 11 emeralds and 5 rubies. The largest diamond in the crown is very famous and is called the Second Star of Africa.

👑 Royal invitations are actually commands and should never be declined. If you get invited to tea with the Queen, you should reply, *I have the honour to obey Her Majesty's command.*

👑 The Queen's handbags are made by a British company called Launer London.

👑 Windsor Castle, one of the Queen's homes, is the largest occupied castle in the world.

The Queen had a special Balmoral Red lipstick created for her to wear during her coronation.

You can only shake the Queen's hand if she offers it to you. You should curtsy or bow when you shake her hand.

The royal household has its own football club!

The Queen's shoes are made by H. & M. Rayne Ltd.

Coronation Street is one of the Queen's favourite TV programmes.

If you want to ask the Queen to tea at your house, you shouldn't send an invitation directly to her. Instead, send it to the Queen's Private Secretary or one of the Ladies-in-Waiting.

The Queen's corgis eat meals prepared specially for them by a chef, such as cooked rabbit or pheasant with crumbled biscuits and gravy. The Queen also feeds them toast and scones!

THANK YOU, EVERYONE

A List of People Who Sent in Jokes

Bloomsbury Children's Books would like to thank everyone who has helped us to compile this book. If you wrote your name down clearly, you'll find yourself listed here (and if you didn't, then don't blame us!).

Extra-special Big Thanks to Books for Students and their school bookshops.

More Extra-special Thanks to:
Huddersfield Daily Examiner
Grimsby Evening Telegraph
West Lancashire Evening Gazette
Bolton Evening News
and their readers.

A

The Abbey School, Suffolk
Abbott, Charlotte
Ackerman, Jenny
Adams, Daniel James
Mrs Adams
Albany Junior School
All Saints Church of England Primary School, Surrey
Almondbury High School, Huddersfield
Anand
Armes, Lucy
Ashby, Bridget
Ashley, Adam
Ashurst, Rachel
Mrs Ashworth
Askew, Claire
Aust, Chloe
Azhakesan, Nicole

B

Baker, Nicola
Ball, Alison
Ball, Kristina
Ball, Rhiannon
Barber, Lucy Anne Margaret
Barker, Katie
Barley, Danielle
Barrow, Craig
Barry, Christopher
Beardmare, Ann-Marie

Bebee, Robert Michael
Bedingfeld, Carly
Bennetta, Paul
Berrisford, Stuart James
Besly, Tim
Bevan, Philippa
Bhatt, Hetal
Bigby, Gemma
Bilan, Sandeep Ricky
Mrs Bilingham
Billiahd, Claire
Binns, Michael James
Mr Birchall
Mr Birchill
Bishops Primary School, Newquay
Bolton Evening News
Books for Students
Mrs Booth
Mrs Boyd
Boylan, Jason
Bradey, Liam
Bradshaw, Marie
Brady, Alice
Brelsford, Jessica
Brown, Matthew
Brown, Sally-Louise
Brown, Samantha
Buckle, Robyn
Buckner, Jack
Mrs Bucton

Bullen, John Martyn
Burbridge, Emma
Burchell, Jessica
Burgess, Kerry Ann
Mrs Burrows
Butt, Jamie
Mrs Buxton

C

Cahill, Rory
Calday Grange Grammar School, Wirral
Caple, Jamie
Carroll, Alexander William Hamish
Carroll, Sophie
Carter, Sian
Cave, Steven Patris Remy
Cerasale, Gemma
Champion, Laura
Chaplin, Dahley
Chapman, Nanette A.
Checchi, Sophie
Christopher
Clark, Stacey Ann
Clarke, Julia V.
Clarke, Nicole L.
Mrs Clubb
Cockayne, Natalie
Coen, Mary
Cole, Christopher
Cole, Thomas

Miss Coleman
Conway, Isla
Mrs Cook
Cook, Richard Alan David
Cooper, Daniel Ross
Cordery, Grace
Coughlan, Jamie L.
Coughlan, Michael
Court Davies, Thomas Edward
Cowan, Tommy
Cowlishaw, Deanna
Coyne, Natalie
Cozens, Jacob
Crawshawbooth Church Primary School
Cuddy, Sam

D

Dame Alice Harper School, Bedford
Danks, Kyle
Darce, Victoria Catherine
Davey, Cecily
Davey, Jenny
Davies, Ben
Davies, Candice
Davies, Carolyn
Davis, Christina
Davies, Gwyn
Davis, Shane
Miss Davison
Davitt, Adam

Dawn, Peter David
Dawson, David
De Claire, Jordan Rose
Delchar, Jonathan
Denman, Kerri
Dever-Champ, George Patrick
Dickenson, Nina
Dinnigan, Natalie
Mr Dobson
Dodsley, Richard
Dominique
Dorrell, Timothy J. H.
Drury, Mark
Mrs Duncan

E
Ebury, Amy
Edros, Stacey
Ellard, Adam
Ellard, Sarah Louise
Ellen
Elliott, Jonathan
Emery, Matthew
Engel, Lynette
Esaw, Olivia
Esmaili, Sohali
Evans, Daniel David
Evans, Jeremy Mark
Evans, Joel James
Evans, Lysia

Evans, Thomas
Evenlode Primary School, Penarth
Everett, Charlotte

F
Fairhurst, Colin
Fanner, Hywel
Findlay, David J.
Flanagan, Michael
Flynn, Daniel Charles
Forbes, Felicity
Ford, Andrew
Foughy, James
Fountain, Jon
Frape, Michael
Freeman, Emma
Furze, Lauren

G
G., Katie
Gallagher, Lee
Gardiner, Sean
Gibbons, Daniel Thomas
Mrs Gibson
Goffin, Emma Jane
Gore, Charles
Gore, Lucy
Gould, Miriam
Mrs Goulden
Graham, Kerry Louise

Graves, Rory
Green, Melanie Sonja Yee
Greensmith, Paul
Gregg, Teleri
Grimes, Lisa
Grimsby Evening Telegraph
Gurner, Oliver

H

Hadden, Michael
Hadddow, Joshua
Hadjan, Lillia
Haigh, Stuart
Mrs Hamilton
Hamilton, Natasha
Hands, Rebecca Jane
Hanetine, Sarah Ashly
Mrs Hardwick
Hargreaves, Michelle
Harrod, Christopher
Hayward, Freddie
Hayward, Hugh
Haywood, Rebecca
Mr Hazell
Hearn, Andrew
Hearson, Jamie
Hebson, Zoe Claire
Mr Henderson
Hicks, Lauren
Hickson, Amy Hannah

Mrs Hill
Hilton, James
Hoare, Tom
Hobbs, Ben
Hodder, Mark
Hodge, Caroline V.
Hodgson, Matthew
Hogg, Zara
Hollis, Robert William
Howarth, Scarlett
Hoy, Nicola
Huddersfield Daily Examiner
Miss Hudson
Hughes, Jonathan
Huish, Clair
Humbertson Comprehensive, Grimsby
Hutchings, Katherine
Hutchinson, Lauren
Hyatt, Jonathan

I

Inwood, Tommu
Ironside, Jennifer

J

Jenning, Gordon
Jennings, Elkie Louise
Jeremy, Fern
Jersey Evening Press
Johnson, Alison

Johnston, Louise S.
Jones, Catherine
Jones, Charlotte
Jones, Lisa Jane
Jones, Louis
Jones, Morgan Frances
Mrs Jones
Jones, Owen
Jones, Theodore
Jordan, Louise
Joyce, Abigail
Joyce, Camilla

K

Kanungo, Angeli
Khalid, Anam
King, Adam
King Edward's Junior School, Bath
Mrs King
King, Samantha Louise
Koomar, Yasmin

L

Lacey, Anthony
Mrs Lambe
Lancaster, Laura
Latham, Alexandra Sarah
Lawrence, Rebecca
Lawson, Kelly
Lea, Chris Peter

Ledgard, Alexandra
Leek, Kirsty
Ley Top First School, Bradford
Lim, Justin
Lloyd Davies, Carys Grace
Lodes, Lisa Ella
Lodge, Kimberley Louise
Long, Jodie
Long, Josh
Long, Tom
Mrs Longbridge
Longford, Matthew James
Low, James

M

MacDonald, Michelle
MacDonald, Ross
McCaughan, Thomas
McCurrie, Wendy
McFarlane, Oliver
McFawld, Michelle
McKaugham, Christopher
McNamee, Luke
Mr Main
Manley, Liam
Mann, Charlotte
Manning, Serena Princess
Mansfield, Natasha
Mrs Mapes
Marg, Casey Louise

Markland, Charles
Marks, Yvette
Mrs Marshall
Martin, Sally
Masters, Abby
Meacham, Hannah
Mee, Matthew
Mrs Mercer
Merchant, Pam, Books for Students
Meredith, Callum
Middlethorpe Junior School, Grimsby
Miller, Jessica
Moira House School, East Sussex
Morgan, Jess
Morgan, Nick
Morgan, Vicky
Morrell, Dawn
Mossaheki, Lydia
Mumry, Emily Jane
Munn, Jack
Munn, Oliver
Munn, Scott

N

Nagji, Heena
Napier, Ian J.
Neadley, Gareth
Neighbours, Andrew
Nelson, George
Nelson, Mark

Nevitsky, Christina
Newman, Alexandra
Nicholls, David
Miss Nicholls
Noel-Shore, Georgina
Nunn, Sarah

O

Oakman, Douglas
Orban, Grant
Outlane Junior High School, Huddersfield

P

Palmer, Jay
Panayis, Nicholas
Parkington, Samantha
Parry, Rebecca
Parsons, Natalie
Pearce, Eleanor
Peat, Lesley, Books for Students
Penley Madras School, Clwyd
Mrs Penry-Williams
Peregrine, Anthony
Peregrine, Sophie
Philip
Pickup, Jade
Pierry, Camilla
Pigott, Jenny
Pinner Park Middle School
Pollock, James Andrew

Potter, Annelise
Pratt, Emma
Prescott, Natasha
Miss Price
Mrs Price
Pride, Matthew
Prothero, Alison
Pugh, Elyn
Pugh, Owen

Q

Quinn-Smith, Charley

R

Rae, Elizabeth
Ramsey Spinning Infants' School, Cambridgeshire
Randall, Alys
Ray-Mainur, Naomi
Mrs Reast
Miss Reevers
Reeves, Andrea Louise
Reeves, Kimberly
Reynolds, Lee
Reynolds, Victoria
Richardson, James
Richardson, Susan
Rider, Nicola
Riley, Victoria Louise
R. L. Hughes Church Primary School
Roberts, James

Robertson, Mark
Mr Roberts-Wray
Robins, Matthew
Mrs Robinson
Rogers, Michael
Rose, Dean
Rouge Bouillon School, Jersey

S

Mr Sackett
St Benet's School, Sunderland
St George's First School, Kidderminster
St Jude's Church of England School, Portsmouth
St Nicholas's School, Blackpool
Salmon, Rachel Jennifer
Sandcross School, Surrey
Miss Sanders
Sariah, Nisha
Savage, Jonathan
Schurr, Emily
Mrs Scott
Scott-Henderdown, Niall
Sealy, Patricia
Seddon, Sam
Settle, Fiona
Shallcross, Vicky
Sharples, Karen
Shell, James
Sherborne Preparatory School
Shields, Gillian

Simmons, Sarah
Miss Simpson
Mrs Simpson
Skipper, Emma Cecilia
Smale, Louis
Smit, Alan James
Smith, Jessica
Mrs Smith
Smith, Phillip
Southam, Terry
Spence, Joseph
Spencer, Louise Elizabeth
Spooner, David
Mrs Spray
Stanbury, Alexandra
Mr Starsiker
Mrs Steele
Stein, Hannah
Stevenson, Ryan
Stirzaker, Rachael
Stone, Matty
Strarbuck, Ben
Stroud, Jessica
Suddaby, Alastair
Mrs Sumner

T

Tait, Emma
Tatham, Emma
Tattersall, Georgia

Taylor, Douglas
Taylor, Laura Joanne
Tennant, Amy
Thomas, Phillip Allan
Thorn, Alistair
Thurmott, Christopher
Thurmott, Suzanne
Tiernan, Ruth
Trickett, Martin
Troth, Thomas
Tucker, Niall
Tueckre, Oliver
Turner, Daniel
Tyrrell, Emily

##

Vanderstok, Hayley Jane

##

Walden, Rebecca
Wateridge, David
Wellesley Wesley, Flora
West Lancashire Evening Gazette
Mrs Whymark
Wittingham, James
Woodcock, Ben
Mrs Wright